Gearing Up
for
Greater Sales

*Helping retail store owners
when their business needs a boost.*

by

John F. Gardner
Founder
Wild Bird Marketplace ®
The Franchise

Other Books by
John F. Gardner

Naturalist's Almanac and
Environmentalist Companion (Six Editions)
Published by: HashMarc/Ballantien Books,
New York, NY

Book of Nature Activities
Published by: Interstate Printers & Publishers

Junior Naturalist's Workbook
Published by: Interstate Printers & Publishers

Environmental Education Curriculum Service
Published by: NYSF Press

Backyard Birdfeeding
Published by: Stackpole Books

Thoughts & Meditations
Published by Look, Read and Do.

The Chronicle of Rendrag
Containing the Wisdom of the fourth happiness

Published by Look, Read and Do..

To the reader:

This book is designed both as a source of information and a workbook in which you should add ideas, concepts and techniques that you find useful in your store operation.

To make the best use of this book you should do a great deal of underlining, adding, editing and expanding.

Make it more than a book - make it your book

Published by:

Look Read & Do ™
4317 Elm Tree Road
Bloomfield, NY 14469

Definition of Business Insanity:

Thinking you'll get
different results
if you keep doing
the same thing
over and over again.

Unknown

CONTENTS:

Part One
Gearing Up for Greater Sales

Key words in retail operations
Learning the fundamentals
Strategy and Tactics

Part Two
Successful Promotions

Promotions used by owners of
Wild Bird Speciality Stores, yet
adaptable for any retail store.

Chapter One:

Key words in retail store operations

Why
Attitude
Image
Growth
Value
Inventory
Mortality

Fact: If you are running *toward* something you have a chance for success. If you are running *from* something failure is most probable.

Question:
Why are you in business ?

_____

_____

_____

_____

_____

_____

_____

_____

_____

_____

_____

_____

_____

_____

_____

_____

_____

Why.

You must begin the process by asking yourself 'Why am I in business?' The key is to determine, if by making the decision to be in business for yourself, you are running toward something (fame, fortune, money, impress your spouse, friends, relatives, etc.) or you are running from something (hard work, a lousy employer, a layoff, fear, etc.).

Nothing can happen until you ask this question and answer it - honestly. Scrape away all the rhetoric, jargon, and hype. Answer in the cold light of reality.

Why am I here ?
With the emphasis on the I word !

Fact: What you say, is what you get.

Question:
What is it you want from this business ?

_____

_____

_____

_____

_____

_____

_____

_____

_____

_____

_____

_____

_____

_____

_____

_____

Hint: Write what you want down on a 3x5 card.
Put it on your bathroom mirror and
read it every morning.

Attitude:

How many times have you said or heard someone say. That won't work at my store. My customers aren't like that. But I have to compete against xyz.

These are negative statements, but more important they are self-fulfilling prophesies. You could just as easily say. I'll try that, if it worked for you, it should work for me. I can do that. These are positive statements and again are self-fulfilling prophesies.

Research has proven over and over again that your attitude and what you say to yourself and to others determines what happens. The bible says 'ask and you shall receive', self-help books say keep a 'positive mental attitude', motivators say develop a 'positive self image'.

I say 'consider a positive, open attitude as a must for success'.

Fact: The immediate, unrehearsed, spontaneous response by 'the man on the street' defines your store.

Questions:

How do you define your store?

_____

_____

_____

_____

_____

_____

_____

How do others define your store ?

_____

_____

_____

_____

_____

_____

_____

_____

_____

Image

If you stop someone on the street and say: When I say (*The name of your store*) what immediately comes to your mind?

What *you* think your store is, really doesn't matter. The only thing that matters is what *your customer* thinks your store is in their mind.

Your store must be known for something, or it will be known for nothing. The only way to determine what your customers think - is to ask.

Based on what your customers tell you, two options exist. One: Strengthen your current focus. Two: Develop a new focus based on customer needs, wants, and desires.

Failure to act - either way, is an invitation to disaster. You must ask often. Listen carefully. Reflect, review, and respond.

Fact: If you're out of sight, you're out of mind. If you're out of the customer's mind, you're out of business.

Keep a record of your mailings to customers

_____

_____

_____

_____

_____

_____

_____

_____

_____

_____

_____

_____

_____

_____

_____

Hint: Monthly mailings are a minimum. Use newsletters, postcards, email. It doesn't matter what. What matters is how often you use them.

Growth.

Your business is built on publicity. Maintained on Advertising. Grows on customer loyalty.

Growth comes from communicating with your customers. Communication is something you must do and you must do it consistently.

Failure to communicate via publicity, advertising, and most importantly directly with your customer, stymies growth and destroys customer loyalty. Failure to keep in touch results in the customer going elsewhere. When your customers start going elsewhere you better start looking for a job elsewhere.

Fact: A $38,000 Chrysler can offer real value. So can a $ 9.95 bird feeder.

Question:
How do you measure value ?

Better Question:
How does your customer measure value?

_____

_____

_____

_____

_____

_____

_____

_____

_____

_____

_____

_____

_____

_____

_____

_____

Value

To be successful you must understand what value is in the eyes of your customers and the people who you want to become your customers.

Value is NOT:

High quality products at high prices, nor is it cheap prices for certain merchandise, nor even prestige behind the product, or how it is positioned in the market or its image.

Value IS:

What your customer thinks it is. In many cases that is first class performance coupled with keeping any and all promises made relating to the product.

Fact: Sure Superstores carry a lot of things. But they don't carry everything. There is a niche out there for you. Find it and work it.

Question:
How do you differ from your nearby Superstore ?

_____

_____

_____

_____

_____

_____

_____

_____

_____

_____

Comment: Our local grocery is big and carries a lot of things But it is now so hung up on it's own brand that I have to go to another store for a brand name bread I like. Guess what, while I am at the other store I pick up lots of other things. Even things the big guy has on his shelves.

Inventory

There is a very old New England Yankee saying. 'You can't sell from an empty cart'. It's as true today as it was 100 years ago.

Find out what the top stores in your retail category carry as inventory. Check the product, quantity, quality and dollar volume.

Then follow these simple inventory rules.

Stock what your customer wants.
Stock the unique.
Stock in depth.

Sell quality.
Sell service.
Ask a fair price.

Hint: Sometimes your customer comes to your store not because of what you sell, but because of what you know.

Fact: Sometimes it is kinder to close the store, than try to save it.

List some ideas explaining how you will avoid GLOS:

_____

_____

_____

_____

_____

_____

_____

_____

_____

_____

_____

_____

_____

_____

_____

_____

_____

_____

Mortality:

Stores go out of business for many reasons. The two most common are:

Catastrophe such as fire, death, earthquake.

Something called GLOS* coupled with insufficient capital resources.

You cannot do much about Catastrophe, but you sure can something about GLOS.

* **GLOS:** General Lack of Sales

Chapter Two:

Learning the Fundamentals

Customer List
Marketing
Sales Pitch
Sales Technique
Invite Customers
Displays
Delight
Promotion
Commitment
Competition
Sell Results

Wish List
Inventory
Existing Customers
Thank You
Advertising
Communicate
Perception
Track Numbers
Actions
Critical Areas
Planning
On its Own

Tip: What good is a mailing list, if no one gets mail.

Last time you listed past performance. This time list what and when you intend to do something.

What   When

_____   _____

_____   _____

_____   _____

_____   _____

_____   _____

_____   _____

_____   _____

_____   _____

_____   _____

_____   _____

_____   _____

_____   _____

_____   _____

_____   _____

_____   _____

Your Customer List:

There is nothing, absolutely nothing, more valuable than your customer list.

It is a diamond mine waiting to yield gems in the form of dollars.

But only if you

Grow it

Work it

Use it

Your customer list is so valuable that some people are willing to pay you money just to use it one time......

Tip: Make sure every marketing program you use includes all five components.

Design a marketing program.
Then test it, then try it.
If it works - do it again.

_____

_____

_____

_____

_____

_____

_____

_____

_____

_____

_____

_____

_____

_____

_____

_____

_____

The Marketing Components:

Every marketing program has five components. This is true for giant companies and main street retailers.

The key marketing components are:

Product - *pick it*

Display - *show it*

Signage - *explain it*

Advertising - *shout it*

Handout - *remember it*

This is a good time to remember,
cross selling is another key to your success.

Tip: It's not the product, it's the story. A well executed sales message couple with a vignette increases sales.

Every product has a story.
What stories do you have ?

_____

_____

_____

_____

_____

_____

_____

_____

_____

_____

_____

_____

_____

_____

"This is a great feeder. I remember the time I was complaining about cleaning seed of the bottom of a tube feeder and Mike Dunn reached into his car and showed me this new . . . . . ."

The Sales Pitch

Every product you sell should have its very own one minute sales pitch and a vignette to go with it.

You sell:

When you know your products.

Can show your customer how that product meets their need.

Have a little story illustrating some one using the product successfully.

Tip: Memorize and use good sales techniques every time and pretty soon people will say you are a born salesperson.

What do you think makes you a good salesperson.

_____

_____

_____

_____

_____

_____

_____

_____

_____

_____

_____

_____

_____

_____

_____

_____

"Do or do not... There is no try."   Yoda

Sales Technique:

In spite of what you may have heard salespeople are not born, they are trained. You can learn to sell.

Like marketing there are key components to any sales technique. They are:

Shopper contact - *hello*

Vignette - *the story*

Sales dialog - *features & benefits*

Closing - *sold*

Cross sell - *anything else*

Follow up - *thanks come again*

Use the six steps consistently and you will soon become that born salesperson everyone talks about.

Tip: Ask your existing customers to invite their friends and neighbors to visit and shop your store.

Question:
How are you going to invite customers to come into your store?

_____

_____

_____

_____

_____

_____

_____

_____

_____

_____

_____

_____

_____

_____

_____

_____

_____

Inviting Customers

You must get customers into the store or else you have no sales.

You can invite customers in

by phone,

by mail,

by word of mouth,

by advertising

But they must be invited.

Hint:
You haven't seen a customer very often over the winter. Then send a packet of 'Forget me not' flower seeds. On the packet put a label with your name address and phone number. Add a note that says something like: 'We haven't seen you in a while - We hope you haven't forgotten us.

Tip: It's not the store - it's the experience.

Question:
What makes visiting your store a memorable experience ?

_____

_____

_____

_____

_____

_____

_____

_____

_____

_____

_____

_____

_____

_____

_____

_____

_____

Displays:

Your store must have dynamic, informative and entertaining displays. Some should enhance a monthly theme and others should change with the season. Keep your displays, fresh, new and exciting.

The marketing potential in creating these 'silent salespersons' includes:

The ability to generate a sound customer base

An opportunity to circulate knowledge of your expertise

Encouraging people to purchase the items they want from people who know what they are talking about

A chance to show off the variety and quality of the merchandise you offer.

Notice I said nothing about price.

Tip: Easy to say 'delight the customer'. But it takes effort to do it. Make the effort.

OK - So what are you going to do to delight your customers

_____

_____

_____

_____

_____

_____

_____

_____

_____

_____

_____

_____

_____

_____

_____

_____

_____

_____

Delight Customers

Going beyond satisfaction to delight is the name of the game in today's retailing.

In today's market you must not only meet a customers needs, but you must exceed those needs.

At one time there was a marketing saying. Quality, Price, Service. Pick any two.

Today the customers not only expects all three but expects even more.

Think like a customer and then answer the question:

"What have you done for me today ?"

Tip: Use promotions wisely, and sparingly so they mean something when they are used.

Make a list of your most successful promotions:

_____

_____

_____

_____

_____

_____

_____

_____

_____

_____

_____

_____

_____

_____

_____

_____

_____

One more time:
A promotion is not a discount.

Promotion:

Advertising can make a brand name number two, but promotions can get it to the top. Ads create attitudes - Promotions get results.

A Promotion is not a discount
A Promotion is not a sale

A promotion is an incentive to do something positive.

A promotion is an incentive designed to get the customer to:

Visit the store
Shop the products
Benefit from the services
Buy the products.

Please: Never, Never make the mistake of thinking a discount or sale is a promotion.

Tip: Shop other specialty stores, you might just find a few neat ideas.

Make like Sam Walton and make a list of things you saw and you feel would go over in your store.

_____

_____

_____

_____

_____

_____

_____

_____

_____

_____

_____

_____

_____

_____

_____

_____

_____

Shop Competition

A smart store owner will shop the competition on at a minimum on a monthly basis.

Then ask themselves:

"Am I leading the way or following?"

If your not leading the way in your segment of the business, you are in trouble.

Leading the way -
The passport to
success.

Tip: Without a commitment you are like a ship without a rudder. Going full speed ahead with no direction.

Give yourself a to do list of how and why you have made your personal and business committments,

_____

_____

_____

_____

_____

_____

_____

_____

_____

_____

_____

_____

_____

_____

Everyone will benefit from
your commitment

Commitment:

Success depends on commitment.
Your commitment must be total and unwavering.

> Make a commitment to your personal needs.

> Make a commitment to your family needs.

> Make a commitment your customers needs.

> Make a commitment to your communities needs.

Always remember: Personal comes first. Family comes right behind it. Then customer and finally community.

Tip: Violate the customer wish list at your own peril.

Today's list of what my customers wants

_____

_____

_____

_____

_____

_____

_____

Tomorrow's list of what my customers wants

_____

_____

_____

_____

_____

_____

_____

_____

_____

Customer Wish List:

Any successful store owner makes it a point to learn what ranks highest on their customers wish list.

They maintain a small note pad by the side of the cash register on which they record their customers special needs and wants. Do the very best you can to meet those needs.

These can be products, services, or support. It the customer feels it is important then you can bet it is.

I still recall the time a customer had an item on her wish list that she needed the next day. Yes I had it for her but I had to send my wife to one of my competitors to get it. Why because a happy customer is a steady customer. I didn't make any money on that sale but she was happy and I kept a very good and profitable customer for a very long time.

Tip: Sell them what you have - that gives them what they want.

Do you really know what the customer really wants when he or she says "I want to buy a ....."

They say they want	They really want
_____	_____
_____	_____
_____	_____
_____	_____
_____	_____
_____	_____
_____	_____
_____	_____
_____	_____
_____	_____
_____	_____
_____	_____
_____	_____
_____	_____

Sell Results:

As you attempt to attract customers and increase your monthly sales you should keep this concept in the forefront of your thinking:

Customers do not buy because of what you are offering. They buy because of the results they hope to get.

For example in the birding business:

Customers buy thistle -
they want Goldfinches.

Customers buy nectar feeders -
they want Hummingbirds

Customers buy stepping stones -
they want a pretty yard

Customers buy gifts -
they want to share their hobby with their friends.

Tip: Ask yourself what have you done to-day to make your customers feel special ?

I remembered their birthday *(I had it keyed in on my customer data base so it showed up when the were checking out.)*

I remembered their favorite suet cake
I remembered their name
I remembered . . . . . .

What do you remember about your customers?

_____

_____

_____

_____

_____

_____

_____

_____

_____

_____

_____

_____

Existing Customers

It is vital that you cultivate your existing customer base.

Your growth and profitability is in their hands.

Statistics show that it takes about five times the money and effort to get a new customer over what it takes to increase an existing customer's annual purchases.

Run the numbers. If your existing customers increased their purchases by just 10% how would that affect your annual sales and profit?

One way to cultivate and increase your customer base is to make your customers feel special.

Tip: Keep in mind an old saying when cash gets tight, and it will - 'There is money lying on the floor' It's called inventory.

I am not waiting until the last minute. My plan for when cash gets tight is to . . . .

_____

_____

_____

_____

_____

_____

_____

_____

_____

_____

_____

_____

_____

_____

_____

_____

Inventory:

Inventory is a reflection of the niche you have carved out for your store. It should speak to your customers as unique, innovative, priced reasonably, and changing.

No discussion of inventory can be complete without reminding you how important it is that:

> You determine a target turnover rate for your store by month and by season.

> You track your inventory turns.

> You keep your inventory in line with sale cycles.

Tip: Don't think customers will refer friends to your store automatically. You must ask your customer to refer your store.

I ask my customers to refer friends by

_____

_____

_____

_____

_____

_____

_____

_____

_____

_____

_____

_____

_____

_____

_____

_____

_____

_____

Say Thank You

You must find ways to consistently thank customer for their business.

You can do this by just saying, "Thanks for shopping here".

By a post card following a major purchase by a customer,

By something as simple as a dish of mints on the counter with a note that says "Our customers (That's you) are worth a mint. Thanks for shopping here."

Remember to ask your customers to recommend you to their friends.

<table>
<tr><td>

WILD BIRD MARKETPLACE®
xxxxxxxxxxxxxxxxx

Be a Birding Buddy

Give the attached card to a friend. When they present the card at Wild Bird Marketplace ® they will receive 20% off on their purchase. Following their purchase bring in this card and you will receive 20% off your purchase.

Card given to: _____
Card expires: xxxxx xxxx
</td><td>

WILD BIRD MARKETPLACE®
xxxxxxxxxxxxxxxxx

You are my Birding Buddy

(To:)_____
Present this card to Wild Bird Marketplace ® and receive 20% off on your purchase. Limited to one card per family.

From _____ your Birding Buddy
Card expires: xxxxx xxxx
</td></tr>
</table>

Tip: If you are not spending at least 8% of gross sales each month on advertising, mailing and promotion you will be hard pressed to succeed.

You need an advertising budget.

Month	% of sale	Ad Budget	Media
_____	_____	_____	_____
_____	_____	_____	_____
_____	_____	_____	_____
_____	_____	_____	_____
_____	_____	_____	_____
_____	_____	_____	_____
_____	_____	_____	_____
_____	_____	_____	_____
_____	_____	_____	_____
_____	_____	_____	_____
_____	_____	_____	_____
_____	_____	_____	_____
_____	_____	_____	_____
_____	_____	_____	_____
Totals	_____	_____	_____

Advertising:

To be successful in retail your advertising must be consistent and focused.

Research has shown it take 27 exposures before the sale is made. Therefore consistent advertising and marketing is critical.

Make it a point to spread your advertising budget over the entire year. Base the amount you spend each month on anticipated monthly sales the next month. In that way your advertising dollars are spent consistently and wisely.

Advertise more when things are slow.

Less when things are good.

Moderately when things are average

But advertise consistently.

Tip: You will be successful if your customers attribute quality and value with your products and services.

Prepare a survey to find out how your customers perceive you operation.

Ask a series of questions.

_____

_____

_____

_____

_____

_____

_____

_____

_____

_____

_____

_____

_____

_____

_____

_____

Perception:

Marketing is a matter of perception.

While it is extremely important what your customer actually gets when visiting your store or purchasing your products; it is what they perceive about you, your store, and your products that really counts.

Make sure your customers and your potential customer perceive your business as providing them with:

Products that adds value to their life.

An experience that makes their day a little better.

An atmosphere that is inviting.

A friendly face, a cheerful smile.

Research tells us that from a customer standpoint it is not so much what a product does, as what a customer thinks and hopes it does. You job is to make their hope a reality.

Tip: Yes it is that important that it is worth repeating. Monthly communications are a must.

Define your plan to communicate with your customers.

_____

_____

_____

_____

_____

_____

_____

_____

_____

_____

_____

_____

_____

_____

_____

_____

_____

_____

Communicate:

Unless you routinely pique your customers's interest they will soon forget you.

You get their interest by communicating news about your store and its products to them on a regular basis.

Your newsletter, postcard, flyer, note, all help you tell your customers you appreciate them.

Your goal should be to have your customers look forward to receiving your communications and then being able to share them with their friends.

Tip: Yes it is true. Actions speak louder than words.

What steps do you plan that will make your store provide what your customers want and need and then come back for more?

_____

_____

_____

_____

_____

_____

_____

_____

_____

_____

_____

_____

_____

_____

_____

_____

Actions:

Your actions should reflect quality products, exceptional service and fair pricing.

Your actions must work to define your customers, their needs and wants.

Your actions must make your store feel, look and respond like a store that meets customer needs.

Want to see what actions can do?
Change things around once in a while and watch customers say, "Gee when did you get that product in?"

Tip: Of all the numbers you can and will check - cash flow is most important.

The numbers:	This month	Last month
Transactions	_____	_____
Margins	_____	_____
Profit or Loss	_____	_____
Inventory	_____	_____
Cash Flow.	_____	_____
	_____	_____

Your analysis of the trend !

_____

_____

_____

_____

_____

_____

_____

_____

_____

_____

_____

Track the Numbers:

Every month you need to track five important numbers. These will tell you how you are doing:

> Transactions
>
> Margins
>
> Profit or Loss
>
> Inventory
>
> Cash Flow.

"Happiness is a positive cash flow"

Tip: Again - twice a year send a question-naire out to your customers asking them to evaluate your store and its operation then take whatever action is required.

List of my key questions.

_____

_____

_____

_____

_____

_____

_____

_____

_____

_____

_____

_____

_____

_____

_____

_____

_____

_____

Planning:

Every store needs a solid growth and development plan. A plan that meets local needs. A plan that is based on continued customer input. A plan that is structured from an ongoing analysis of your data base of information. A plan that reflects your personal and your business goals.

Some things to consider

1. Annual Summary of the business
2. Past performance analysis..
3. Current Industry Analysis.
4. Analysis of your Customers.
5. Analysis of your Competition.
6. Plan for next year

Tip: Experience tells us that those five things differentiate you from other stores.

List your personal evaluation of your store and name the things that differentiate you from your competition.

_____

_____

_____

_____

_____

_____

_____

_____

_____

_____

_____

_____

_____

_____

_____

_____

_____

_____

Review the critical areas:

Evaluate your store using the following criteria.

Ambiance

Convenience

Selection

Service

Price sensitive items.

This is my list. Consider what your list might be. Better yet ask your customers.

Fact: None of these marketing tools work when used all by themselves. But together they work wonders for your business.

Notes:

_____

_____

_____

_____

_____

_____

_____

_____

_____

_____

_____

_____

_____

_____

_____

_____

_____

_____

_____

On its own:

Direct mail doesn't work on its own.

Telemarketing doesn't work on its own.

Free seminars to customers don't work on their own.

And for certain, advertising doesn't work on its own.

You must focus your attention on a combination of marketing tools and you'll find that they all work when you use them as a overall strategy.

Chapter Three:

Strategies and Tactics

Relationships
Returns
Second Sale
Inside Signs
Show & Tell
Law of Seven
Law of Three
Price Sensitivity
Sales Technique
Why people don't buy

Tip: You will find that when it is all said and done customers buy from your store because they like you. It's that relationship that counts.

Notes:

_____

_____

_____

_____

_____

_____

_____

_____

_____

_____

_____

_____

_____

_____

_____

_____

_____

_____

_____

Build a Relationship:

You can increase sales by building a relationship with your customers based on trust, fairness, openness, honesty, convenience and value.

If you can manage to make this day a little brighter by treating your customer courteously and fairly he/she will very likely return time and time again.

Returning customers are a bonanza. They increase your annual sales and require little or no marketing expense.

Consider this. A one time customer spends $50.00 and that is great. A returning customer coming in weekly spending $20.00 each week - that is fantastic.

Cultivate a relationship with customers and you will be successful.

Yes it's OK to ask that a receipt be shown and a thirty day limit be imposed. Sale items are sold 'as is', no returns, no exchanges.

A customer return story:

I recall a customer coming in and asking to return a bag of Niger seed. I opened the bag, ran the seed through my fingers and told the customer the seed was old and dried out. I then offered her a full replacement of the seed - on one condition. She had to go back to the store where she bought it and tell the owner it was not good. She was embarrassed to say the least. I assured her I really wanted her to have good seed. No -I did not accept her money for the new seed. Sure I could have charged her for the seed, but I made the decision not to have her pay. Why because I knew that by my action she would become my customer . She did and I made a lot of sales over a lot of years.

What would you have done ?

_____

_____

_____

_____

_____

Maintain a 'no questions asked return' policy:

Sure there are people who will abuse the privilege. Sometimes you will get stuck with an expensive product you cannot resell *(at least at full price)*.

But remember if someone has a bad experience they tell seven other people who each in turn tell five other people. In turn they tell another five people. We're now up to one hundred and seventy five people. It takes a lot of advertising dollars to overcome that bad publicity.

Meanwhile make sure you post your return policy for all to see and make it a policy that customers can appreciate.

Tip: A 'bounce back' will help stimulate that second sale. There are many kinds of 'bounce backs'. Consider the ones you remember and use those for your customers.

Write down some bounce backs you remember and pick the best ones and use them in your store.

_____

_____

_____

_____

_____

_____

_____

_____

_____

_____

_____

_____

_____

_____

_____

That second sale:

This is one of those maxims you want to remember for as long as you are in business.

They are not a customer
until you get the second sale.

The concept is that you don't have a real customer until you have a satisfied, repeat customer. Most salesmen operate on the basis that you can sell anything once. It's the second sale that really counts.

During the first sale, go for that next visit, that next sale.

Here is where the idea of a Bounce Back in every bag proves its value.

Tip: *A photo of a product being used by a persons makes a great inside sign.*

Mrs Jones
had great success
with her bluebird-
feeder - You will
too.

Who can you ask to share a success story ?

_____

_____

_____

_____

_____

_____

_____

_____

_____

_____

_____

_____

_____

Increase Sales with Inside Signs:

The Point-of-Purchase Advertising Institute tell us that 70% of all purchases were affected by inside signs.

Inside signs allow you to help the customer know the features and benefits of a product, where the product is located, and its price. Use inside signs to inform and entice customers to buy.

Consider non standard ideas in your signs. Framed prints, framed posters, framed newspaper ads *(blown up)*, framed testimonial letters, etc, etc.

Many newspapers will make a copy of your ad and mount it if you ask.

Tip: As part of your selling process make sure the customer gets to hold the product.

What ways can you get your customer involved in the buying and selling process?

_____

_____

_____

_____

_____

_____

_____

_____

_____

_____

_____

_____

_____

_____

_____

_____

No more show and tell:

The days of show and tell are long gone in the retail business.

You must get your customer involved in the selling process. When I was in the Bird seed business we did this by getting the customer to reach into a bin and see how clean and fresh the seed really is. Or had them lift the lid on the feeder to see how easy it is to fill. Or let them listen to the tape before they bought it.

Today selling is an active process not a passive event.

Now you know why the telephone company used seven numbers for local phone service.

Here are some famous logos using seven words or seven sylables.

Takes a licking and keeps on ticking
Timex

Without music, life would be a mistake.
Nietzsche

Smooth seas do not make skillful sailors.
Author : Frédérick Jézégou

The Good Life at a Great Price.
Sears

Try some examples for your store:

_____

_____

_____

_____

_____

_____

_____

Use The Law of Seven:

Memory experiments conducted more than 100 years ago *(and repeated many times since then)* revealed that the human short-term memory can hold only about seven items at once.

When preparing an ad, poster, bulletin board or announcement to attract customers to the store make sure you get the main part of your message across in seven words or less.

Note the samples on the previous page.

Consider: Why don't genies grant just two wishes?

You tried some 7's now try making some 3 part logos for your store.

_____

_____

_____

_____

_____

_____

_____

_____

_____

_____

_____

_____

_____

_____

_____

_____

_____

_____

_____

And now the Law of Three:

In your efforts to increase sales remember the other rule, the rule of three. A series of three produces a rhythm that causes a positive and pleasing sense of completion and fulfillment.

Don't overwhelm the customer with too many choices.

Three choices seems to be the right number.

Good-Better-Best

Small-Medium-Large

Food-Shelter-Water

Size-Color- Price

Tip: Everything at Wal-Mart isn't sold for less but those key price sensitive items are. For example check 60 watt bulbs. Nowhere are they cheaper. Then check out what they charge for printer ink !

Compare your competition

Item	Them	Us

Pay attention to
price sensitive products:

Your not a discount house or hopefully even a standard retail store. Your a specialty store. However you still need to know the six or eight price sensitive products you have in your store.

Research has shown that if these six or seven price sensitive items are priced right in your store the customer automatically assumes the <u>entire</u> store is priced to their advantage.

When I ran my store I identified 6 items I considered price sensititive. Do you know the price senstive items in your store?

Price sensitive = The price every competitor charges.

Tip: The job of the order getter is to identify the customers needs, and then fill those needs.

Evaluate your own sales technique and those of your staff.

_____

_____

_____

_____

_____

_____

_____

_____

_____

_____

_____

_____

_____

_____

_____

_____

Constantly evaluate your sales technique:

There are three types of sales personnel.

Order handler
(check out person)

Order taker
(takes the order and makes suggestions)

Order getter
(uses creative selling efforts).

You need to be an order getter and hire and/or train only order getters.

Refer back to page 33 for suggestions
regarding sales techniques

Tip: Take time to understand the reason people don't buy, then implement sound strategies to neutralize their impact and get a higher percentage of sales.

Notes:

_____

_____

_____

_____

_____

_____

_____

_____

_____

_____

_____

_____

_____

_____

_____

_____

_____

_____

Why people don't buy !

There are five reasons why people don't buy:

   1. Wrong seller.

   2. Wrong product.

   3. Wrong price.

   4. Wrong time.

   But most often

   They were never asked.*

* Believe it or not, most salespeople are so busy explaining the features and benefits that they forget to ask the customer "Will this do the job for you?" "Shall it take it up to the check out counter while you continuie shiopping?"

Part Two

Successful Promotions used by owners of Wild Bird Speciality Stores.

Following are several promotions designed to help you get more customers to purchase more products, more often, at higher profit margins. They can be adapted to almost any kind of retail store

A Birdy Buck:

Print up some 'Birdy bucks' with expiration dates. For every $10.00 a customer spends give them one (1) Birdy buck to be redeemed later.

Treat a 'Birdy buck' like you would a real dollar. For example if a customer comes in and buys something for $12.87 they could pay for it with a $10.00 bill and three (3) Birdy bucks. Their change would be .13 cents.

If you do the math you will find out this is a very small discount for the benefits it provides.

Good for $ 1.00 toward the purchase of product at xx store.

One Birdy Buck

Bird house plans for the kids:

You may want to set up a display showing how to make a milk carton bird house.

Granted you can't sell houses, but you can generate interest and provide a way to open the cross selling conversation.

Also the parents and grandparents will think you are a great retailer who thinks of their children and grandchildren in an educational and fun way.

You couldn't buy the word of mouth advertising you will get from this activity

Birds and Golf.

When I was operating the franchise we had a store that sold 32 Coveside Bluebird houses to a customer for a golf outing.

(Naturally they put store tags on the boxes and the houses and as a result had additional inquiries)

Bird houses and Golfing are a natural combination. Look into it in your area.

This book is available from
UMass Extension Bookstore in Amherst, Ma

A Description:

Next to each one of your displays you should have a short description of the qualities the particular product.

For example with a bird bath your description might be:

"A pedestal bird bath is a versatile bird bath. It is used by most birds and drippers and misters can be attached."

Or

"Mister attachments attract Hummingbirds because they allow the Hummingbirds to bathe on leaves that have been misted."

Posters are available from www.naiwbs.com

Don't forget your nearby ????

We have stores that have forged a working relationship with their nearby Nature Center , Butterfly House, or Education Center.

This kind of relationship is good for both you and the organization. It also shows the community that you support worthwhile community activities.

If you haven't forged a relationship with your nearby group - do it today.

Summer Suet:

Remember suet is now a year around product. We had a store who sold twenty cases of suet on one <u>summer</u> weekend.

How? By using a flyer offering a special promotion for a case of suet. In addition he wrote up a nice publicity release explaining the benefits of summer suet. Plus he made up a poster using his computer that promoted summer suet use in the backyard

The Bird Feeding Station:

Every store should have an example of a Bird Feeding Station - tube feeder, platform feeder, suet feeder, baffle, bird bath and greenery to represent shelter.

On a nearby table set up a pair of Binoculars, a Field Guide and an open Notebook. Write dates, times, bird species and numbers in the Notebook. *(For example, September 4, 1998, 8:00 a.m. Chickadee 10, Bluebird 4, September 5, 1995, 10:30 a.m. Bluebirds 6, Junco 3, and so forth).*

This will stimulate customers to either set up a comprehensive station or add to their backyard feeding station.

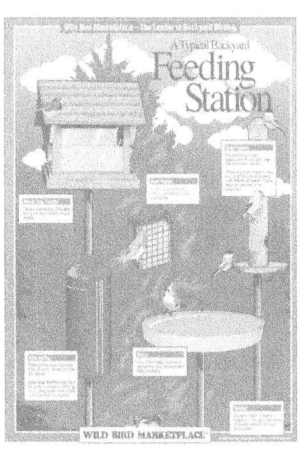

Check out our full color feeding station poster.
naiwbs.com/posters.htm

The Bear Feeder:

One of the stores had a customer bring in a feeder that a 'bear' had crushed in its mouth.

The store owner hung it by the front counter and asked people to guess what happened to it. If they guessed correct they got a free two pound bag of black oil.

People had a lot of fun and it was a good attention getter.

Photo from
www.Bearsmart.com

On the Field Trip:

Whenever you or someone from your store staff take a field trip have them take along pair of binoculars or a spotting scope along. Encourage people to use them during the walk.

 Then pass out your business card with a note on the back inviting people to visit your store.

The Expert is Available:

One of the best things you can do to promote your store and increase sales is to offer talks, demonstrations and workshops to local civic groups, garden clubs, scouts, and schools.

As your reputation grows (and it will) so grows your store sales.

The expert is available today

The Bounce Back:

We touched on the 'Bounce Back' earlier, but it is worth repeating. The "Bounce Back is something that you give to the customer, after the sale has been rung up. Something that will entice the customer to either come back into the store to buy again, or will encourage the customer to recommend you to their friends.

There are all kinds of bounce backs you can use.

A coupon good for 10% off their next purchase. A business size card reminding the customer that 'We redeem our competitors coupons on the same products or products of equal value'. A poster for the refrigerator that reminds the customer of your store, your hours and your phone number. A 'Birding Buddy' card. A candy 'mint' with the statement 'Just to remind you, your business is worth a mint to us'.

No customer should leave the store without a bounce back......

Joint Ventures:

Talk to other merchants in your complex and see how you can complement one another. The following is an actual joint venture one of our Wild Bird Marketplace stores did with a bakery across the street.

Example:

You advertise *" Got Cake - We Do".* *Buy a suet cake for the birds and receive a 'sweet treat coupon' for a free cupcake at John's Bakery.*

Meanwhile John's advertising went. *Buy a dozen cupcakes and receive a 'bird treat coupon' for a suet cake at Ann's wild bird store.*

It was a win -win both stores got new customers.

Visiting Groups:

Invite the local Audubon chapter, garden club, conservation group, bird club or other civic group, into your store for a presentation.

Let them set up a table to tell about their activities and solicit memberships.

Give new members of the group a 'discount card' for future purchases.

This activity costs you very little, but in terms of good will the gains are fantastic.

Vendor Support

Many stores have used their vendors to come in and do a workshop on a Saturday for their customers.

For example when I was running my store in up state New York I invited my binocular salesperson to come in and offer exterior cleaning and alignment inspection for customers.

I was surprised by the number of customers who came in, and I was also surprised how easy it was to do an exterior cleaning and interior inspection. Customers really appreciated the workshop. Store visits increased as people learned we were a source of not only binoculars but information about binoculars.

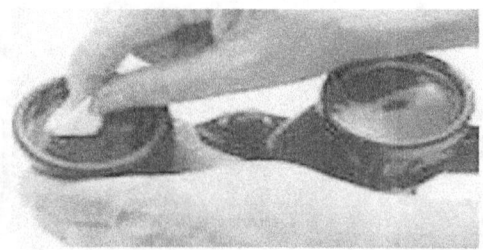

Friend of - The Friends of ...

Many nonprofit groups have an auxiliary group known as 'The Friends of ...'

One way to increase sales and word of mouth is to invite leaders of the Friends of Group into the store to tell your customers about their project.

Pass out their brochures, write them up in your newsletter. Then ask them to do the same for you.

I did this with a group that had a walking trail on an old railroad bed. It was one of those win win projects.

Friends of the Brier Bush Nature Center in Pennsylvania

The place to go -
If you want to know.

Make your store the place to go if you want to know about any birding, conservation, gardening or community activity.

Make sure your store has a wildlife watching community bulletin board available for your customers use.

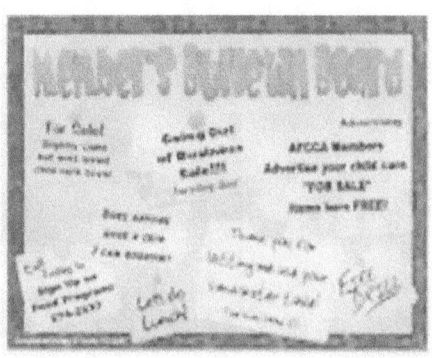

Workshops:

Invite a local craft person to come in and demonstrate his/her speciality.

Consider something like painting bird houses, making door wreaths, Christmas Pine Cone ornaments.

In addition ask around to see if there are any authors in your sales area that might like to come in for a book signing ?

These kinds of activities draw large numbers of participants and as a result sales increase.

**Gearing Up
for
Greater Sales**

*Helping retail store owners
when their business needs a boost.*

By John F. Gardner
Founder
Wild Bird Marketplace -
The Franchise

Congratulations:

I first learned about this promotion when I had my name in the newspaper for giving a talk at a local school.

A man in our town watched the local paper for notices of people who are honored or do something special. He then sent them a note congratulating them. I later learned he had been hired by two local business firms to carry out this activity for them. I immediately hired him to do it for the Nature Center where I was executive director.

People love this kind of thing and will thank you for your kind-ness, plus they tell their friends, and shop your store.

Birding Hot Line.

If you can't afford to underwrite the local birding hot line as part of your advertising program, at least make up a business size card that lists the local 'Birding Hot Line' telephone number.

Pass these cards out to anyone and everyone interested in birding. The word of mouth advertising you get from this activity will surprise you. Especially when people come in to ask for the Birding Hotline number.

**OUR LOCAL
BIRDING HOTLINE**

Phone: xxx-xxxx
Email:
xxx@xxxx.com

Brought to you by
xxxxxxx

Punch Cards:

Punch Card Promotions can help your build regular clientele and foster goodwill with your customers. There are a lot of creative uses for punch card promotions.

Here are some suggestions: Buy ten get one free. You have seen these cards almost everywhere. They are popular because they work.

Consider other types of punch card uses. For example Dollar Per Punch. Make up a card with fifty blocks instead of ten. For every dollar the customer spends punch a block. A full card is worth $ 5.00 on the customers next purchase.

Half Full Punch. Make up a card with twenty punches, but offer the free product at punch number ten and again at punch number twenty.

The Birdy Bucket:

This promotion is common with many stores. Some use milk jugs, some plastic baggies, others buckets. A few of my stores tried it using what we called a 'birdy bucket' and it worked just find. Especially for older folks who did not want to carry a 20 lb. bag.

Begin by offering your customers a 5# Birdie Feed Bucket that is refillable and has a "punch" card stuck to the lid which gets stamped with each refill. After 10 refills the next bucket of seed is free.

The bucket is like an ice cream tub with a handle and complete with label and punch card costs about $1.06 each. They are very popular with customers.

Dislocate an item.

Try putting some product somewhere where it is not expected and watch the results.

When I tried it I was surprised at how many people said "When did you get that in?", when in fact I had it in inventory for several months. Months not weeks.

This photo is an example of a display concept we used called Theme marketing clusters.

Similar birdhouse products (houses, books, flyers, etc.) clustered on a homostote backgrounds.

Appeal to customers value system.

For example you should create a display that appeals to grandparents value system. This means they should emphasis education, etiquette, and family fun.

You need to take time to show Grandparents the value of the products in your store, and how their grandchild will benefit from it.

Grandparents spend a lot of money on their grandchildren and you need to get your share. Their world is not made up of just buying their grandchildren toys, but introducing them to their hobbies. Help Grandparents accomplish that in your store.

Special Value

Implement the concept of 'special value product' in your store. Set up a small permanent *(nicely decorated)* table in the back of the store. Pick one, and only one, product category as 'This Weeks Special Value'. Prepare a sign explaining the many features and benefits of this 'Special Value Product'. Then price it accordingly.

In the beginning you will need to tell customers about 'This Weeks Special Value', but quickly they will learn to look for it and will support it with sales.

```
Special
Value
```

Remember this is not a clearance table it is a 'special value'

You're worth a mint.

This is a very common promotion especially in the hotel and motel business. You put out a dish *(birdbath)* with wrapped mints in it.

The sign says;

Please take one -
Your business is worth a mint to us.

Caution: I did this once with candy kisses. A lady came in the door, shouted. "Just stopped by for a Kiss John."
Customers eyes turned and stared directkt at me.

Good thing my wife loves and trusts me.

Coupons.

Avoid them if you can. But redeem your competitors every time.

You will quickly find that your customers will love you, meanwhile you will drive your competitor crazy.

Pick up
some
Savings

Match-making:

Keep a supply of the business cards of merchants in your complex on your back counter. Then if someone asks if you can recommend someone for something. Give out the card.

On the back of the card place a label saying "Referred by John at Wild Bird Marketplace." That way the customer remembers who helped and the merchant remembers who referred the customer.

It's a win-win.

Easy to Shop

Put small notes and photographs on products that are hard to access or need explanation.

This helps the customer shop even when your busy with another customer.

This may seem like a simple little thing, but you will be surprised how much customers appreciate learning about various products without having to ask someone else.

We can recommend this book for young birders

Butterfly promotion

Give away a free butterfly bush (also attracts hummingbirds) *(buddleja)* with the purchase of any oriole, hummingbird, or butterfly feeder or hibernation box.

I know of stores that have been using this promotion for years and years. Just when they think it has run it course, customers begin asking about it in the Spring. It is not uncommon to sell 75 feeders during a weekend when this promotion is running.

Check with a local grower or the internet, most times a grower will prepare butterfly bush seedlings for you. But you need to contact them in pleanty of time to grow the seedlings.

Migration Watch

Hold an Annual Spring Migratory Watch with customers.

Beginning in mid-February post a bird count board. When a customer sees an unusual migratory bird, they come in and add the sighting to the board. Customers report every bird from yellow warblers to hawks, vireos to oven birds.

Use cross selling techniques when customer come in.

*Spring moves north about 7 miles a day.....
Go to http://www.learner. org/jnorth/ to track Spring migration*

Be different

One way to have unique and different products in your store is to create special products. Try this: Find some old license plates from your State. Then have someone make up birdhouses using these plates for the roof.

This makes your store unique and your products different.

From: www.runnerduck.com

Be part of your community:

In many towns you can be a sponsor of a Little League team for just $250.00.

Think about it. Your store name on the back of little kids shirts for several months during the spring and summer. Every time they win, or even lose, your name gets mentioned.

Plus your the good guy or gal who supports the community.

Jacob my favorite little league star

We can do that:

How many times have you seen signs that say NO. Well how about a sign on your counter that says YES !

Need change for the pay phone
we can do that

Need your purchase wrapped
we can do that

Need to borrow a pen
we can do that

Need something special ordered
we can do that

We can do that

Be part of the hobby:

If customers don't come to you - then go to them.

Take time to attend local bird club meetings, field trips and activities. Get out there and let the birders know you exist.

Sell yourself,

Your store,

Your products.

Hand out your business card.

Have a contest:

If you want to attract customers, have a contest.

It could be a photography contest, it could be a kids drawing contest, it could be an in store quiz.

Get all questions correct and receive a prize - a poster, a small bag of seed, or a book, etc.

Give out lots of prizes. If you have a photo or drawing contest notify the local media on prize award day.

Reindeer Food:

At Christmas hand out little bags of bird seed with a tag (see below) on them that says Reindeer Food.

At Easter make up little packets of cracked corn with a tag that says "Easter Bunny Food". The week before Easter put them in a basket on the counter for people to take.

Reindeer Food

Tis the night before Christmas and most years you leave milk and cookies for Santa. This year leave some food for his Reindeer.

Instructions:
1. Wait until Christmas eve.
2. Open this bag and sprinkle Reindeer food on your lawn.
3. Hop in bed and listen for Santa
4. Close your eyes and have happy dreams.

Contents: Enought Reindeer food for 8 tiny reindeer

Sidewalk Sale:

Have a sidewalk sale each Spring and Fall. Use the sale to eliminate slow moving inventory. But be sure to put a few good items in the sale to make customers really appreciate it.

This booklet is available at www.naiwbs.com
It explains the formula used by a wild bird store owner to do in excess of $9,000 over a spring weekend.

Samples, more samples and still more samples:

The public loves free samples.

Give out free samples of your most popular product if possible.

Give out samples of products given to you by your vendors

Or even give out inexpensive promotional products purchased from specialized vendors.

> # FREE Sample
> # Try It
> # Before you
> # buy It

Bird Walks:

We had a store in Pennsylvania that hired a local birding expert to offer bird walks to their customers every two weeks during the Spring and again in the Fall..

They had the walk begin and end at the store. They provided free coffee and donuts before the walk and free cold juice after the walk.

The publicity and goodwill worked wonders. Sales increased after the sale, and on some occasions, when people were waiting for the walk to begin, seed sales increased.

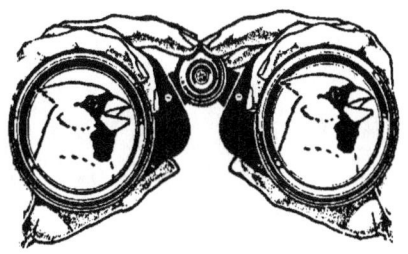

The Christmas Gift:

Guy who operated a store just outside of Philadelphia sent his key customers a Christmas letter with a coupon that could be redeemed for - a small gift box with something like a one pound of Deluxe seed, or a handmade bird edible tree ornament, or chocolates in the shape of butterflies, birds and sunflowers, plus a discount coupon for use between January 1st and March 31.

This made a great Christmas Gift and stimulated January sales.

Take One:

People who are into birding and gardening are information hungry.

Be sure you have a good supply of informative handouts for your customers.

Consider such things as: Bird house preference chart, Seed preference chart, Gardening for wildlife, Planting for birds, etc.

Purchase some plastic pamphlet holders and scatter them throughout the store. Customers will appreciate the information flyers in them and will tell their friends about them.

Full color Posters are available at www.naiwbs. com under the category business publications

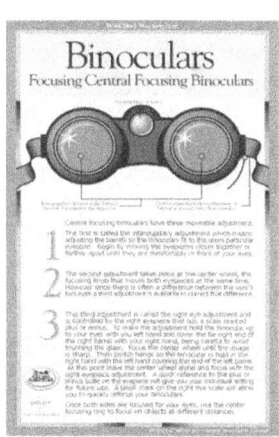

Customer Appreciation:

Customer Appreciation Days are one of those legitimate sales promotions that can be run once maybe twice each year.

They are an excellent way to increase sales in slow months, or reduce inventory when cash is short.

Finch Days:

In early spring when the Goldfinches are in the process of changing from their dull winter color to spring breeding color is a good time to hold Finch Days.

Emphasis should be on finch feeders and Nyjer (thistle) seed.

I held one of these finch days in February one year. It was the biggest one day sale in the history of the store. We filled up our parking lot and the hardware store's next door. The line of customers streatched down one row and up the next to the checkout area. What a day it was!

Gift Baskets

Some stores have had great success with Gift Baskets. So much so that some suppliers actually sell them to wild bird stores.

When making up gift baskets go through the store and choose items that correlate, pick a theme. For example Doves, gather up all dove related items in the store, books, notepaper, millet, pictures, etc. You could place a dove ornament nestled within the basket.

Remember the tissue paper liner and ribbon for decoration. This is a time to just be creative.

Bird Feeder Trade In Sale

This promotion is a gem. It works every year.

The best display you could possibly make is simply to get hold of an old battered up and broken feeder and place it next to a brand new top of the line feeder. Then place a "It's time for a Trade-In!" poster above these two feeders.

The secret to the success of this promotion is advertising. People usually don't think about the possibility of trading in their old feeder for a new one. They figure that they would just have to go out and buy a new one which people will put off until their old bird feeder is nothing but a pile of kindling. This promotion gives people an option, so spread the news!

Check Lists

If your not providing your customer with a check list of products you are missing a great opportunity to increase sales and help your customers.

These can be made up on your computer, printed locally and put out for customers.

Here are some samples

Feeders:
☐Platform
☐Hopper
☐Tube
☐Ball
☐Hummingbird
☐Oriole
☐Suet

Other
☐Nest Boxes
☐Roost Boxes
☐Field Guides
☐Binoculars
☐Spotting Scope
☐Camera

Water Features
☐Birdbath
☐Pond w/waterfall
☐Mister
☐Dripper

Fall Truckload Sale

Everybody, or at least everybody I know in the bird food business, does a Fall Truck-load Sale. If for some reason you don't, it's time to rethink your overall marketing plan.

There are a few things you need to keep in mind when doing a Truckload sale.

1. Keep the pickup time short. With prices changing almost weekly you don't want to be selling tomorrows higher priced seed at today's price.

2. Limit the amount any one customer may buy and put away for the future, for the same reason.

3. Make the process quick and simple.

I have a book available based on a 64 page manual my wife Trudy used since 1974 with nonprofit groups who used a Truckload Seed sale as a fund raising program. Go to www.naiwbs.com. Click on business publication for information

Christmas Tree for the Birds

This promotion is as old as the hills. Suffice to say a good poster is the key.

This poster is availabe from
www.niawbs.com/posters

Squirrels- Problems and Solutions
A focus on Baffles

The purpose of this promotion is to look at a potential annoyance customers could be having at their bird feeding station. You want to point out to your customers that your store can provide solutions.

A good display is key. Hang a variety of squirrel baffles in the store. You may simply want to string baffles from the ceiling with fishing line at different levels. Attach pole baffles to standing feeders. Adjust the height of each pole to different length for a more attractive display.

It's a good idea to prepare a handout   for your customers around the theme. "Baffle the Squirrels?" I would also attach a tag on the baffle stating its features and benefits as well as its cost.

The Children's Barrel

Take a plastic or tin can and fill it with any seed from broken bags. Put some lunch bags and a small scoop with a sign saying

Children up to the age of 12 may take one full scoop of wild bird feed, a gift from us for their backyard bird friends. All other's 60 cents a pound.

Kids think it's fun and parents and grandparents will actually take time to bring in the kids to get a scoop.

Guess what - The parents and grand-parents buy something while the kids get their free scoop.

Buckets available from Duncraft

NOTES

The Author

John F. Gardner was born in Brooklawn, New Jersey on November 10, 1933. He graduated Magna Cum Laude from Glassboro State College in New Jersey and received his Master's Degree from Eastern Connecticut State University. He is best known for his work in the field of Backyard Birding and Nature Center and Small Museum management. He is an author and lecturer on topics of retail operations, marketing and self improvement.

In addition to writing Gearing Up for Greater Sales, he is the author of five editions of "The Naturalist's Almanac and Environmentalist's Companion" published by Balantine Books, "A Book of Nature Activities" published by Interstate Printers and Publishers, "Backyard Birdfeeding" published by Stackpole Books, and other books and materials on nature study, environmental education, self improvement, marketing and management.

Mr. Gardner presently lives in Bristol New York with his wife Trudy. He is available for work shops, lectures and seminars.

www.ingramcontent.com/pod-product-compliance
Lightning Source LLC
Chambersburg PA
CBHW071717170526
45165CB00005B/2054